To my mommy and daddy. Thank you for always believing in me.
Daddy, thank you for always telling me that I am beautiful,
smart, and that I can do all things through Christ.

ISBN: 979-8-9865519-0-6

For more books, visit us online at lyricj.net

I'm Beautiful, I'm Smart, and
I Can Do All Things

By Lyric Johnson

I am beautiful.

I am beautiful because God created me.
He never creates anything ugly or bad.
My hair, skin, or size does not define my beauty.
Instead, it shines from within.

Look at yourself in the mirror and say, "I'm beautiful."

1 Peter 3:3-4

I am smart.

God gives me knowledge. I learn a lot from reading my Bible
and listening to my parents, teachers, and pastor. I pay attention
to what is being taught because I know it will help me in the future.

Be smart by listening to God and using the lessons
and good advice that people give you to better your life.
Intelligence is your superpower. It helps you make good choices.

Proverbs 2:6

I am patient.

Sometimes things do not happen as fast as I would like them to. When I see cookies baking in the oven, I am ready to eat them immediately. But I know that I have to wait until they are fully cooked and my mommy takes them out of the oven.

Patience can sometimes be hard, but it is worth it. When you are playing outside, and someone is on the swing that you want to get on, have patience and wait your turn. You may even meet some new friends.

Galatians 5:22-23

I stand up for what I believe in, and I am not afraid to do it alone.
I did not get this strong overnight. God and my family help me
grow every day by encouraging me, teaching me, and guiding me

You can be strong, too. Wherever you go and whatever you do, know that God is with you. He wants you to have strength and courage. Stand up and stand out!

Joshua 1:9

I am capable.

I can accomplish any task I am asked to complete.
Whether it is tying my shoes, brushing my teeth, or fixing my lunch,
I can handle whatever task I am asked to complete. I may be small,
but I can handle HARD things.

When you are facing difficult assignments,
just know that God can help you through them.
He is walking with you and helping you when
something seems impossible.

Hey friend, **you are capable**. Never forget that.

🕊️

Mark 9:23

I am independent.

Cleaning my room and getting ready for school all by myself makes me feel really proud. But even though I can do things on my own, I still need God's help. He gives me the confidence and strength to do these things and more.

Philippians 4:13

I am brave.

I am brave because God lives in me. I take him everywhere I go.
God can help us be brave. God can help calm our fears.
He is our rock, comforter, protector, and safe place.

If you are feeling alone or afraid, just know that God
is always with you. He will be there for you at all times.
Just talk to him. Even in your dark room he is there.
If you ever feel afraid, ask God to help you
and just like that, **he is there for you.**

Psalms 23:4

GOD, please help me not to be afraid!

I am kind.

I treat people the way I would like to be treated and would never want to hurt anyone's feelings. God is kind, and I want to be just like him.

You can be kind like God, too.

Do nice things for people in need. Help your family around the house. Random acts of kindness also make people feel really good.

Proverbs 11:17

I am unique.

There is no one else like me. My laugh is contagious,
and my smile is as bright as the sun. I love being myself.
My differences make me irreplaceable.

It is okay to be different. This makes you one of a kind,
unique, and powerful. There can never be another you.
So, smile big, laugh out loud, and be yourself.
The world needs your individuality.

Jeremiah 1:4-5

I am inventive.

I have a big imagination, and I love creating new and fun things. I am a fashionista. Sometimes I take different clothes and put them together to make my own style. I am in total amazement when I see my visions come to life.

You can be inventive, too. You were created to give something new to the world. Whatever your gifts and talents are, God will give you wisdom about how to create something.

Proverbs 8:12

I am healthy.

I choose nutritious foods to eat like cherry tomatoes and juicy cherries. Candy and other sweet treats are delicious, but I know they are not good for me all of the time. I also exercise. I stretch daily with my sister and work out with my daddy.

Make sure you select healthy foods to eat and exercise daily so you can be healthy, too. A healthy life is a better life.
Get up and get moving!

🕊️

1 Corinthians 6:19-20

I am a leader.

Instead of being a follower, I choose to lead with boldness and courage. My words and actions are powerful, and I am not afraid to stand up for what I believe in, even when my friends disagree.

There is a leader in you, too.
You can do anything that you desire, so be yourself and follow Jesus, not the crowd. He will make you the head and not the tail.

🕊️

1 Timothy 4:12

I am victorious.

I live a victorious life. I can overcome all obstacles because I walk in victory and can conquer anything.

Christ loves you so much.
He will cheer you on, and you will be able to defeat anything that you face.

Romans 8:37

I am determined.

I can accomplish anything I put my mind to because God has promised to help me. When I face hard things, I pray and ask God for assistance. Then, I get up and try again. I may not always get it right the first time, but I know that with God, I will eventually accomplish my goal.

There is nothing that you cannot do when God is with you. Stay focused and don't lose hope. You are stronger than you think, and with God's help, you can do it all.

Galatians 6:9

I am loved.

My mommy, daddy, brothers, and sisters care for me.

They show me that they love me with their words and actions.
Most importantly, God loves me. I feel his love every day.
He protects me, watches over me, and guides me in all of my ways.

God loves you, too. He protects and watches over you.
God's son Jesus gave his life just for you. He is always
with you and will never leave your side.

You are Loved.

Ephesians 4:2

About the Author

Lyric Johnson is an entrepreneur, speaker, model, author, and actress. She enjoys music, dance, reading and math. When she is not writing in her journal and creating music, she loves to grace fashion runways in the Atlanta area, spend time with her family, and hang out with her friends. Her company, Lyric J., seeks to inspire and encourage youth around the world through the word of God. To learn more about Lyric and her upcoming events, follow her on Instagram and Facebook.

www.lyricj.net   Facebook: @lyricj2013   Instagram: @_lyricj

Made in the USA
Columbia, SC
13 October 2024